D0532090

Thinking Critically: Video Games and Violence

Andrea C. Nakaya

ReferencePoint Press®

San Diego, CA

About the Author

Andrea C. Nakaya, a native of New Zealand, holds a BA in English and an MA in communications from San Diego State University. She has written and edited numerous books on current issues. She currently lives in Encinitas, California, with her husband and their two children, Natalie and Shane.

For more information, contact:
ReferencePoint Press, Inc.
PO Box 27779
San Diego, CA 92198
www. ReferencePointPress.com

Picture Credits:
Thinkstock Images: 9
Maury Aaseng: 15, 22, 29, 35, 42, 48, 56, 61

LIBRARY OF CONGRESS CATALOGING-IN-PUBLICATION DATA

Nakaya, Andrea C., 1976-
 Thinking critically : video games and violence / by Andrea C. Nakaya.
  pages cm. -- (Thinking critically)
 Includes bibliographical references and index.
 Audience: Grade 9 to 12.
 ISBN-13: 978-1-60152-590-1 (hardback)
 ISBN-10: 1-60152-590-7 (hardback)
 1. Internet and children--Juvenile literature. 2. Video games--Juvenile literature. 3. Children and violence--Juvenile literature. 4. Internet--Safety measures--Juvenile literature. I. Title.
 HQ784.I58N35 2014
 004.67'80835--dc23
                                                      2013026248

Contents

Foreword

"Literacy is the most basic currency of the knowledge economy we're living in today." Barack Obama (at the time a senator from Illinois) spoke these words during a 2005 speech before the American Library Association. One question raised by this statement is: What does it mean to be a literate person in the twenty-first century?

E.D. Hirsch Jr., author of *Cultural Literacy: What Every American Needs to Know*, answers the question this way: "To be culturally literate is to possess the basic information needed to thrive in the modern world. The breadth of the information is great, extending over the major domains of human activity from sports to science."

But literacy in the twenty-first century goes beyond the accumulation of knowledge gained through study and experience and expanded over time. Now more than ever literacy requires the ability to sift through and evaluate vast amounts of information and, as the authors of the Common Core State Standards state, to "demonstrate the cogent reasoning and use of evidence that is essential to both private deliberation and responsible citizenship in a democratic republic."

The Thinking Critically series challenges students to become discerning readers, to think independently, and to engage and develop their skills as critical thinkers. Through a narrative-driven, pro/con format, the series introduces students to the complex issues that dominate public discourse—topics such as gun control and violence, social networking, and medical marijuana. All chapters revolve around a single, pointed question such as Can Stronger Gun Control Measures Prevent Mass Shootings?, or Does Social Networking Benefit Society?, or Should Medical Marijuana Be Legalized? This inquiry-based approach introduces student researchers to core issues and concerns on a given topic. Each chapter includes one part that argues the affirmative and one part that argues the negative—all written by a single author. With the single-author format the predominant arguments for and against an issue can be synthesized into clear, accessible discussions supported by details and evidence including relevant facts, direct quotes, current examples, and statistical illustrations. All volumes include focus questions to guide students as they read each pro/con discussion, a list of key facts, and an annotated list of related organizations and websites for conducting further research.

The authors of the Common Core State Standards have set out the particular qualities that a literate person in the twenty-first century must have. These include the ability to think independently, establish a base of knowledge across a wide range of subjects, engage in open-minded but discerning reading and listening, know how to use and evaluate evidence, and appreciate and understand diverse perspectives. The new Thinking Critically series supports these goals by providing a solid introduction to the study of pro/con issues.

Video Games and Violence

In July 2011 Norwegian Anders Behring Breivik set off a series of bombs in downtown Oslo, killing eight people. He then drove to nearby Utoya Island with a bag full of weapons and proceeded to calmly and systematically shoot sixty-nine people dead and wound hundreds of others. Most of the victims were youths who were attending a summer camp there. At his trial Breivik testified without emotion about how he shot as many people as he could, firing more bullets at those who tried to play dead or were injured and could not escape. He claimed that his goal was to kill all six hundred campers on the island.

At the trial Breivik also revealed that he played the video game *Call of Duty: Modern Warfare 2* as part of his training for the shooting. In addition, he said that at one time prior to the shooting he spent up to sixteen hours a day playing *World of Warcraft*, another violent game. These revelations immediately sparked renewed debate about the effects of video game violence, a topic that provokes intense disagreement in the United States and around the world. Critics say that violent acts such as Breivik's are often precipitated by violent game play, while others argue that claims such as this are not backed by evidence. While not everybody plays violent video games for sixteen hours a day as Breivik did, these games are a popular form of entertainment for people of all ages. Yet, as the Breivik case illustrates, there is continuing disagreement over how they impact society.

Increasingly Realistic Violence

Society's perception of video game violence has changed dramatically in the past fifty years. As technology improved, games became increasingly violent and realistic. *Spacewar!*, one of the first video games that involve players attempting to destroy something, was created in 1961 and consists of two starships that try to shoot each other. The ships can fire torpedoes, increase or decrease their speed, and turn. The graphics are simple lines. In comparison, today's violent games are far more realistic. For example, writer and editor Dan Nosowitz writes about a demonstration he attended for *Sniper Elite V2*, a game that came out in 2012. Nosowitz says the game designers conducted extensive research to make the game feel realistic to players. He says, "They consulted medical experts, ex-military snipers, photography of real-life gunshot victims and x-rays of bone fractures." He describes the result in one part of the game when the player fires at a Nazi sniper:

> The camera rotated back behind the bullet to follow it as it got closer and closer to the enemy. Then it reached the enemy's face. Suddenly the Nazi's skin peeled back, like a Venetian blind rolling up, snapping backwards over his skull. I saw the bare, perfectly clean bone, the teeth, grinning and eerie, the spinal column beneath with its visible path of nerves. The bullet splattered through the cornea, shattered the bones of the eye-socket and cheek, broke through the blood vessels at the back of the eye, burst backwards through the brain cavity and punched a hole in the back of the skull.[1]

Research shows that a large number of people play violent video games such as this one. While the Entertainment Consumers Association reports that the majority of video games have no violence in them, statistics indicate that those games that are violent account for a significant percentage of game sales. According to the Entertainment Software Association (ESA), in 2011 seven of the ten top-selling video games contained significant amounts of violence, including *Call of Duty: Modern Warfare 3* and *Assassin's Creed: Revelations*.

Youths and Violent Games

Research also indicates that many youths play violent video games. For example, in 2012 the American Psychological Association (APA) published the results of a four-year study involving more than five thousand US teenagers. Thirty-two percent said they had played *Spiderman II*, 12 percent had played *Manhunt*, and 58 percent had played *Grand Theft Auto III*. All three of these games are violent. For example, in a review of *Manhunt* the website Gamespot says, "The game itself unflinchingly depicts intense graphic violence, the likes of which you might expect from a slasher movie."[2] ESA data reveal that most violent play occurs with parents' knowledge: the organization reports that parents are present 90 percent of the time when games are purchased or rented and that 91 percent of parents say they pay attention to the content of the games their children play.

Conflicting Research

How video game violence affects people is an extremely controversial topic. Some people maintain that it is harmful, while others insist that it is not. Hundreds of studies have been conducted in an attempt to answer the question, yet even the studies have proved to be controversial. Critics disagree about the validity of study designs and offer differing interpretations of the results. As National Public Radio science correspondent Shankar Vedantam says, "The irony is that scientists who think the games are harmful, and those who think they're not, are both looking at the same evidence. They just see two different things."[3]

Assessing the effect of violence is difficult. While video games might impact how people think and act, numerous other factors—including personality traits and family influences—also influence thoughts and behavior. Iowa State University developmental psychologist Doug Gentile compares the effects of game violence with the effects of smoking. Cigarette smoke has an impact on the individual smoker, but the effect is not always noticeable. He says, "Two-thirds of smokers don't get lung cancer because they have enough protective fac-

> "[Creators of the violent game *Sniper Elite V2*] consulted medical experts, ex-military snipers, photography of real-life gunshot victims and x-rays of bone fractures."[1]
>
> —Dan Nosowitz, a writer and editor.

The effects of violent video games, especially on young players, are uncertain. Some researchers warn that such games, played often and over an extended period of time, can lead to aggressive or violent thoughts and behavior while others say that links drawn between video games and violence or aggression are not scientifically valid.

tors. But if you open them up and look at their lungs, you'll see that it was still influencing them all along."[4]

Some people contend that video game violence actually has benefits for players. They maintain that by engaging in violent play, people release frustrations in a harmless way, reducing the likelihood that they will commit violence in the real world. It is also argued that exposure to game violence can be beneficial to youths because it helps them learn to deal with violence or fears that they might experience in the real world.

Regulating Game Violence

For as long as there has been violence in video games, there have been people trying to regulate it, particularly to keep children and teens from being exposed to it. The first widespread public protest over video game violence occurred in 1976 with the release of *Death Race*, in which cars run over stick-figure characters to win points. Hitting a stick figure causes it to scream. Due to public outrage *Death Race* was pulled off the market after selling only a small number of games. In 1993 Senator Joseph Lieberman proposed federal regulation in response to the violent games *Mortal Kombat* and *Night Trap*. *Mortal Kombat* is a fighting game, well known for a move called "Fatality," whereby a player can use a variety of violent moves to kill an opponent who has already been defeated. *Night Trap* is a horror adventure game where the player fights vampiric creatures. In response to proposed regulation, the video game industry instituted its own regulation system in 1994, which is still used today.

> "The irony is that scientists who think the games are harmful, and those who think they're not, are both looking at the same evidence. They just see two different things."[3]
>
> —Shankar Vedantam, science correspondent for National Public Radio.

The ratings system is overseen by the Entertainment Software Rating Board (ESRB), which assigns ratings and enforces industry-adopted guidelines for advertising games. The ratings divide video games into six categories: Early Childhood (C), Everyone (E), Everyone 10+ (E 10+), Teen (T) for ages 13 and up, Mature (M) for ages 17 and up, and Adult (A) for ages 18 and up. In addition to these ratings, video game labels contain descriptions that explain in more detail why a game has been given a particular rating. For instance, some games might carry this explanation: "Blood and Gore—Depictions of blood or the mutilation of body parts." Others might have this description: "Violent References—References to violent acts." Digitally distributed games are not subject to the same requirements or enforcement as packaged or boxed games; however, the ESRB strongly encourages their makers to follow its guidelines.

Despite the video game industry's self-regulation, there are repeated efforts to institute government regulation. The most recent attempt—to ban the sale of extremely violent games to children in California—was declared unconstitutional in 2011 by the US Supreme Court.

Relevant to Everyone

Controversy over video game violence is ongoing, and based on statistics about game play, it is a topic that is relevant to most Americans. Statistics show that people who live in the United States have a good chance of being exposed to video game violence at some point in their lives. In 2012 the market-tracking company NPD Group reported that approximately two-thirds of Americans play video games. The percentage of young people is even higher; in 2011 NPD found that 91 percent of Americans aged two to seventeen play video games. A significant percentage of the games being played contain violence. So the average person has a good chance of playing a violent game at some point in his or her life. By thinking critically about video game violence, players and others can better understand the potential risks and benefits of this activity.

Chapter One

Does Video Game Violence Cause Violent Behavior?

Video Game Violence Causes Violent Behavior

- The connection between game violence and violent behavior is well supported by research.
- Playing violent games arouses the body into a state where violence is more likely.
- Video games teach violence through active participation and rewards.
- Violent game play desensitizes individuals to violence.

The Debate at a Glance

Video Game Violence Does Not Cause Violent Behavior

- There is no scientific evidence that violent video games cause violent behavior.
- Studies of game violence have questionable validity because they have too many flaws.
- A comparison between the occurrence of violent game play and the violent crime rate suggests that games actually reduce violence.
- Violent games prevent violent behavior by letting people harmlessly release aggression.

Video Game Violence Causes Violent Behavior

"Regardless of research design or conservativeness of analysis, exposure to violent video games . . . [is] significantly related to higher levels of aggressive behavior."

—Anderson is a professor at Iowa State University and well known for his research on video game violence.

Craig A. Anderson et al. "Violent Video Game Effects on Aggression, Empathy, and Prosocial Behavior in Eastern and Western Countries: A Meta-Analytic Review," *Psychological Bulletin*, vol. 136, no. 2, 2010, p. 162.

Consider these questions as you read:

1. How strong is the argument that video game violence causes violent behavior? Which piece of evidence is the most persuasive? Why?
2. Do you agree with the argument that because violent games stimulate the body's fight-or-flight response they make violent behavior more likely? Why or why not?
3. Can you think of an example of a time when you learned a particular skill through video game play? How did the video game help you learn?

Editor's note: The discussion that follows presents common arguments made in support of this perspective, reinforced by facts, quotes, and examples taken from various sources.

In 2012 the *Journal of Experimental Psychology* published the results of a study investigating the effects of violent video game play. Seventy participants played either violent or nonviolent games for twenty minutes a day, for three consecutive days. Researchers tested their aggression by allowing them to blast another person with loud, unpleasant noise through headphones. They also asked participants questions designed to reveal aggressive thoughts and feelings. The researchers found that participants who played violent games displayed more aggressive behavior, thoughts, and feelings than those who played nonviolent games—and that this increased with each day of violent play. This study is only one of many that demonstrate how violent video games can lead to violent behavior.

A Link Well Supported by Research

A large body of scientific research shows a link between violent game play and violent behavior. In 2012 well-known social psychologist and video games researcher Brad J. Bushman conducted a comprehensive review of existing research. In his examination of 136 studies of video game violence involving more than 130,000 participants from around the world, he found strong support for a link between violent games and violent behavior. Bushman found that violent games can cause violent behavior in many different ways. He says, "These studies show that violent video games increase aggressive thoughts, angry feelings, psychological arousal (e.g., heart rate, blood pressure), and aggressive behavior. Video games also decrease helping behavior and feelings of empathy for others."[5] He also found that the effects were consistent for both males and females, regardless of age or country of origin.

"Violent video games increase aggressive thoughts, angry feelings, psychological arousal . . . and aggressive behavior."[5]

—Brad J. Bushman, researcher on the effects of video games.

Other researchers analyzing existing data have come up with the same conclusions. For example, another major review of existing research was conducted in 2010 by prominent game researcher Craig A. Anderson and a number of other experts. The researchers used the results from more than 130 research reports to conduct their own analysis of the link between violent games and violent behavior. Based on the data from all these studies, they concluded that exposure to violent video games is unquestionably related to higher levels of aggressive behavior and to increased aggressive thinking. The researchers conclude, "We believe that debates can and should finally move beyond the simple question of whether violent video game

Violent Games Have a Strong Impact on Behavior

Certain behaviors are known to have a high chance of causing certain effects—aspirin is known to reduce the risk of heart attack, asbestos increases the risk of developing cancer, condom use reduces the chance of a person's developing HIV. To show the strength of such cause-and-effect correlations, researchers have come up with a statistical formula that generates something called an effect size—the higher the effect size, the higher the correlation. All of the items listed at the top of the chart are widely considered to have statistically significant cause and effect correlations. Researchers have used the same formula to understand the correlation between video games and various types of negative behaviors—aggression, desensitization to violence, an increase in hostile thoughts. As can be seen in the chart, the cause and effect relationship between video games and these behaviors has an effect size just as statistically significant as more familiar and more studied topics.

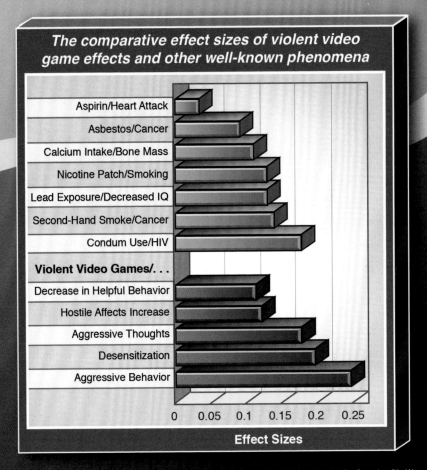

The comparative effect sizes of violent video game effects and other well-known phenomena

Source: Craig A. Anderson and Wayne A. Warburton, "The Impact of Violent Video Games: An Overview," in Wayne Warburton and Danya Braunstein, eds., *Growing Up Fast and Furious: Reviewing the Impacts of Violent and Sexualized Media on Children.* Annandale, Australia: Federation, 2012, p 87.

play is a causal risk factor for aggressive behavior; the scientific literature has effectively and clearly shown the answer to be 'yes.' Instead," they argue, "we believe the public policy debate should move to questions concerning how best to deal with this risk factor."[6]

Media Effects Are Widely Accepted in Society

In addition to the research specifically focused on video games, a large body of research shows that media influences thinking and behavior even when it is not violent. As the Media Violence Commission of the International Society for Research on Aggression points out, this is the premise behind advertising. Such influences can also be seen in other forms of media. The commission states:

> The multibillion dollar advertising industry flourishes on the assumption that showing people media advertisements will make them more likely to buy the advertised product. Airlines train prospective pilots on flight simulators to teach them virtual flying skills before allowing them to fly a real plane. Limiting sexually explicit material from being shown at times when children might be watching reflects the belief that such media contents adversely affect young people's development. These examples show that media contents of different sorts are accepted to have an impact on how people feel, think, and act in real life.[7]

With so many widely accepted examples of media influence, it defies common sense to argue that video game violence does not affect people, too.

How Game Play Causes Violence

One way video game violence causes violent behavior is through the physical effect it has on the body. When facing a dangerous situation in the real world, a person's body reacts by preparing to fight or run away—a reaction known as the fight-or-flight response. Researchers have found that violent game play elicits this same response, arousing the body into a state where violence is more likely. Journalist Jeanne Nagle describes the body's reaction. She says, "Violent content in entertainment media gets the heart beating rapidly, the blood flowing faster, and the lungs pumping quicker." She adds, "Our bodies release chemicals, like adrenaline and cortisol, in preparation for either running away or staying and fighting."[8] All of these physical reactions prime the body for aggressive behavior and thus make it more likely that a person will behave violently. While the situations in video games do not pose true threats to players, Nagle points out that the human body is often unable to recognize this. She says, "When we sense violence in our environment, our bodies do not fully differentiate between fantasy and reality."[9]

Games also encourage violent behavior because players are learning violence thorough active participation. Anderson and researcher Wayne A. Warburton explain that active participation is a very effective way to learn because players must pay close attention to what they are doing, and this means they are more likely to remember the behaviors they are engaging in. They say, "The combination of interactivity and frequent rehearsal is a potent one for learning. In essence, this is a key reason that video games are such powerful tools for teaching pilots, astronauts and soldiers their core skills."[10] Just as pilots learn how to fly by repeatedly rehearsing through a video game simulation, people can also learn to engage in violent behavior by such repeated rehearsal.

In addition, games encourage violence by rewarding violent behavior. One way people learn how to act in society is through the consequences of their actions. Actions that reap rewards are more likely to be repeated, whereas actions that offer no rewards or that lead to negative consequences are less likely to be repeated. Violent games reward violent behavior, for example, through praise or by awarding extra points or allowing players to pass to higher levels. For instance, in the *Grand Theft Auto* games players are rewarded for numerous types of violent behavior, including killing people and blowing up cars. *Grand Theft Auto III*—released in 2001—caused public outrage over the ability of a player to pick up a prostitute and pay her for sex, then kill her to get the money back. Laura Davies, a child and adolescent psychiatrist in San Francisco, explains that such rewards affect the way people understand violence. She says, "A huge part of discipline and development is understanding consequences." She says, "Video games like Grand Theft Auto turn the consequences into positives. You kill a prostitute and get points, you're rewarded."[11]

A Major Risk Factor

While the causes of violence are multifaceted, extended exposure to video game violence significantly increases the chances of real-world violence. Doug Gentile explains that violent behavior results from a combination of factors. Violent video games, he says, "are one risk factor for aggression among many, and it takes several risk factors, combined with few protective factors, to move someone from mild aggression to serious physical violence."[12] Thus, many people who play violent games will not commit real-world violence because they have no other influences or personality traits predisposing them to violence. However, for those who have additional risk factors, violent games help push them to violence. For example, in 1999 Columbine High School students Dylan Klebold and Eric Harris went on a shooting rampage inside their school. Prior to the shooting, the two teens spent large amounts of time playing violent video games. However they also had other risk factors that likely contributed to their violent behavior. Harris had complained of depression, and both had allegedly been the victims of repeated bullying by classmates.

> "[Violent video games are] one risk factor for aggression among many."[12]
>
> —Doug Gentile, developmental psychologist from Iowa State University.

Violent video games are an important cause of violent behavior. Playing violent games primes the body for violence and also teaches and reinforces violent behavior. This is well supported by research and widely accepted by society.

Video Game Violence Does Not Cause Violent Behavior

"The myth that video games cause violent behavior is undermined by scientific research and common sense."

—Gallagher is president and CEO of the Entertainment Software Association, the trade association that represents US computer and video game publishers.

Michael D. Gallagher, "Video Games Don't Cause Children to Be Violent," *U.S. News & World Report*, May 10, 2010. www.usnews.com.

Consider these questions as you read:

1. Because the laboratory is not the real world, some say laboratory studies of video game violence do not prove anything about real life. Do you agree? Why or why not?
2. How strong is the argument that the declining violent crime rate means video games are not the cause of violence? Explain your answer.
3. Can you think of a time when playing a video game has helped you deal with feelings of stress or anger? Why do you think the game was helpful?

Editor's note: The discussion that follows presents common arguments made in support of this perspective, reinforced by facts, quotes, and examples taken from various sources.

There is no scientific evidence that video game violence causes violent behavior. While many researchers claim their work shows such a link, most studies are so flawed that they prove nothing about the effects of video game violence beyond the laboratory. A 2009 study by researcher Christopher Barlett illustrates some of the problems. To study the effects of video game violence, Barlett recruited ninety-one university students and had them play either the violent video game *Mortal Kombat: Deadly*

Alliance or the nonviolent game *Hardhitter Tennis* for fifteen minutes. The idea was to test the participants' levels of aggression after the game play.

Studies like this one have serious constraints, however. No ethical researcher would ask study participants to commit real acts of violence or aggression toward one another. Instead, researchers had to find other ways to measure aggression. In this case, participants were instructed to put hot sauce in a cup. They were told that the cup would be given to another participant who did not like hot or spicy foods, and that participant would have to consume it all. (Nobody actually consumed the hot sauce in this study.) Researchers found that study participants who played *Mortal Kombat* gave fellow participants larger amounts of hot sauce than those playing the tennis game. From this, researchers concluded that the violent game had made them more aggressive.

This study is similar to others that have looked into the effects of video game violence. Largely as a result of studies such as this, researchers have concluded that video game violence causes violent behavior. However, this example reveals an important flaw: those conclusions are based on artificial situations that may or may not reflect real life.

Not Like the Real World

Playing video games in a laboratory situation is not the same as playing them in real life, so study results cannot be used to make conclusions about games and violence in the real world. In a 2013 book, video game experts and teachers from the IT University of Copenhagen caution, "The laboratory is not similar to everyday situations." They state, "The majority of laboratory studies do a very bad job at replicating the phenomena they want to study. . . . Usually, players are not in charge of how long they play, what they play, or how they play."[13] For example, in the Barlett study participants were assigned one of two games and played for fifteen minutes, while in reality most players have more game choices and spend far longer playing a game. In addition, while researchers try to disguise the real purpose of their research, participants are aware that their actions are being observed and analyzed, which is likely to impact their behavior. Because of all these problems, the results of a controlled research experiment on video game play are not proof of what happens in a real-life situation of game play.

Another problem with video game research is that it is impossible for researchers to show that playing a violent game is the direct cause of a person's acting or thinking violently. Many variables influence a person's thoughts and actions. To identify one factor as a cause of behavior requires eliminating all other factors—and video game researchers have not been able to do this. Researchers, for instance, must take context into account. As the authors of *Understanding Video Games: The Essential Introduction* explain, "When someone plays a video game, the activity cannot be understood without considering the context he is playing in." For example, "The player may have friends hanging around, be alone in a big house, or just stopping by the local game café."[14] Players are also influenced by numerous other factors including genetics, gender, and a history of family violence.

Leading researcher in the field of video game violence Christopher J. Ferguson, a professor of psychology and criminal justice at Texas A&M International University, argues that constructing a valid study to determine the possible influence of video games on behavior is exceedingly difficult because so many variables are at play. He believes that a large number of the existing studies have been poorly constructed and their results are thus invalid. For example, he says, "Assessments [of aggression and violence] in the realm of video game violence studies have too often been shockingly and embarrassingly poor."[15] Therefore, in his view, the scientific proof of a connection between game violence and aggression has not been shown.

> "Assessments [of aggression and violence] in the realm of video game violence studies have too often been shockingly and embarrassingly poor."[15]
>
> —Christopher J. Ferguson, professor of psychology and criminal justice at Texas A&M International University.

Examining the Crime Rate

Interestingly, as the hysteria surrounding video game violence has risen in recent years, statistics show that violent crime in the United States has

No Link Between Video Games and Violent Crime

If video game violence is a cause of violent behavior, then increases in video game playing should be accompanied by increases in crime. However, statistics reveal that the opposite is true. Since 1990, video game sales in the United States have increased dramatically, while the violent crime rate has decreased. It is thus unlikely that game violence— or any part of video game play—is a cause of violent behavior.

■■■ Violent crimes in the US (m)   **▬▬▬ North American Software Sales ($bn)**

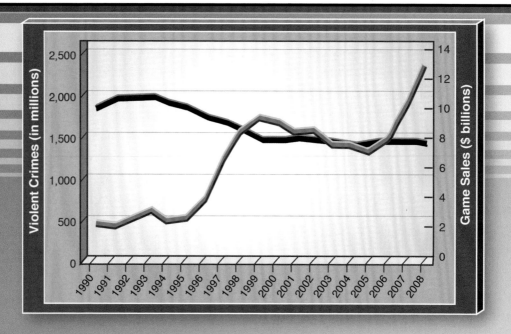

Source: Nicholas Lovell, "If Video Games Cause Violence, There Should Be a Correlation Between Game Sales and Violent Crime, Right?," *Gamesbrief* (blog), August 6, 2010. www.gamesbrief.com.

actually decreased. This suggests the absence of a correlation between violent video games and real-world violence. If such a link existed, surely it would be reflected in crime statistics. Yet statistics show the opposite to be true. According to FBI data, in 2011 violent crime (which includes murder, forcible rape, robbery, and aggravated assault) was 15.5 percent lower than the 2002 level. The Entertainment Software Association reports that while the crime rate has fallen, video game sales have grown dramatically, more than tripling between 1998 and 2011. Concludes Michael D. Gallagher, president of ESA: "The evidence makes a mockery of the suggestion that video games cause violent behavior."[16]

In fact, one writer suggests that violent video games might actually bear some responsibility for the declining violent crime rate. *Forbes* writer Erik Kain says, "Why are violent crimes down? It may not have anything to do with video games. Still, it's also possible that relatively cheap, accessible, and time-consuming electronic diversions keep people occupied who might otherwise be out getting into trouble." He theorizes, "Maybe the more time people spend playing games, the less time and motivation they'll have to go out and commit crimes."[17]

> "The evidence makes a mockery of the suggestion that video games cause violent behavior."[16]
>
> —Michael D. Gallagher, president of the ESA.

In a 2011 research paper Michael R. Ward, an economist at the University of Texas, Arlington, and two other researchers also suggest such a possibility. They analyzed the crime rates in a number of different communities following surges in violent video game sales. The researchers found that following an increase in the sale of violent games there was actually a decrease in crime, especially violent crime. They conclude, "Our evidence finds robust evidence that violence in media may even have social benefits by reducing crime."[18]

Preventing Violence Through Catharsis

Like Ward, proponents of another theory, called the catharsis theory, also believe that violent video games may actually benefit society. According to catharsis theory, people do have negative feelings such as aggression that they need to deal with in some way, and playing violent video games allows them to release their aggression in a harmless way. In a 2010 article in the *Review of General Psychology*, public health consultant and media researcher Cheryl K. Olson discusses her research of media use by students and finds support for the catharsis theory. She says that many students report using games—particularly violent ones—to manage stress and feelings of anger. For example, she quotes one player as saying, "Getting wrapped up in a violent game, it's good. 'Cause if you're mad, when you come home, you can take your anger out on the people in the game."[19]

A study by Brad J. Bushman and other researchers, reported in 2013 in *Psychological Science*, also supports the theory that people use violent games to help them release negative feelings such as aggression or frustration. Study participants were given a multiple-choice exam that included a copy of the answers, allowing them to cheat. Before some participants were able to complete the exam though, researchers acknowledged their "mistake" and took away the answers so that cheating was no longer possible. Following the exam, participants read about a number of video games and rated how much they wanted to play them. Students who had the opportunity to cheat taken away from them were more likely to choose violent games, suggesting that they were attracted to violent games as a way to release the frustration of not being able to cheat. According to the researchers, a second experiment involving the opportunity to steal quarters yielded similar results, with the participants who were denied the chance to steal quarters being more attracted to violent games.

As can be seen in the research and through an examination of crime rates, violent video games do not cause violent behavior. In fact, there is evidence that violent video game play may actually benefit society by reducing crime and helping people release violent feelings without actually harming anybody.

Chapter Two

How Does Video Game Violence Affect Youths?

Video Game Violence Harms Youths

- Violent game play teaches youths to use violence in the real world, too.
- Youths who play violent games have an exaggerated perception of how much violence exists in the world.
- Repeatedly playing violent games desensitizes youths to violence.
- Numerous major scientific organizations agree with the position that violent video games are harmful to youths.

The Debate at a Glance

Video Game Violence Does Not Harm Youths

- Exposure to imaginary scenarios that are both violent and scary can help children learn to deal with violence.
- Violent game play can empower young people.
- Through violent game play, youths engage in many types of beneficial social interactions.
- Playing violent games allows youths to safely release aggression without actually harming anyone.

Video Game Violence Harms Youths

"Significant and repeated exposure to violent video games is not healthy for young people."

—Bushman is a professor of communication and psychology at Ohio State University.

Brad Bushman, "Video Games Can Spark Aggression," *New York Daily News*, March 20, 2013. www.ny dailynews.com.

Consider these questions as you read:

1. How persuasive is the argument that violent game play teaches youths that violence is an acceptable way to behave in the real world? Explain.
2. Do you agree with the argument that violent game play desensitizes youths to violence? Why or why not?
3. The American Academy of Pediatrics and other organizations warn that violent games pose a risk to youths. How do the positions of these organizations impact your opinion on this subject? Explain your answer.

Editor's note: The discussion that follows presents common arguments made in support of this perspective, reinforced by facts, quotes, and examples taken from various sources.

In a recent article journalist Brandon Keim describes the game *Call of Duty: Modern Warfare 3*, a game that is played by many youths. He stresses that game play is both realistic and violent. Says Keim, "You're submerged in a sewer, watching soldiers herd prisoners at gunpoint through the nighttime streets of a near-future dystopia. A few inches in front of you, just below eye level, raindrops dapple the water, a bit of graphical realism that subtly reinforces the game's first-person perspective. *You are there.*" According to Keim, not only do players feel like they are really there but while there they actively participate in many violent acts. He says, "Twelve minutes later, you've gunned down 21 people and one dog. Most fall amidst head-shot geysers of blood. You've also killed some unknown number by rocket launcher or machine gun, their deaths lost in the haze. Every now and then, blood spatters onto the screen, as if in your eyes."[20] While many people regard games like *Call of Duty: Modern Warfare 3* as mere entertainment, there is evidence that such realistic and violent game play has effects on youths beyond merely entertaining them and may actually be causing significant harm.

Learning Violence

One of the harms of violent video games is that they teach players to use violence in the real world. Childhood is a time of learning about the world and how to behave in it. One way children learn is through observation; they watch how others behave and then repeat that behavior in their own lives. For example, when children hear their parents say "please" when asking for something, they learn that this is appropriate behavior. The Media Violence Commission of the International Society for Research on Aggression explains this learning process. It says, "The human brain, like a few other primate brains, is uniquely wired to imitate what humans see being done. Imitation occurs in infants, in toddlers, in children, and in adults, but young children are particularly susceptible to imitate what they see. It is not an exaggeration to say, 'Children see, and children do.'"[21]

Video games also teach children lessons about what is normal and appropriate. The commission explains, "Children make inferences about what they see being done and develop normative beliefs about the appropriateness of specific behaviors. If they see someone solving a social problem by behaving aggressively, they store away in their memory a script for behaving that way and a belief that it is acceptable to behave that way."[22] Thus when children are exposed to violence in video games, that violence may be stored in their memory as a normal and appropriate way to act in the future.

Violent video games can also give youths an exaggerated perception of how much violence exists in the world, which may significantly impact the way they live their lives. Psychologists call this phenomenon the "mean world" syndrome. Exposure to high levels of violence in the media, including video games, leads children to think that the real world is a much more violent and dangerous place than it is. Author David Ropeik describes the mean world theory. He says, "If we think the world is a 'mean' and violent and unsafe place, the kind of world we see again and again in both the news and so much entertainment media, we live our lives accordingly. We buy guns to protect ourselves. . . . We live in gated communities." He says, "In a violent and threatening world we are readier to fear 'others.' We mistrust more."[23]

An Effective Teaching Tool

Children learn from many different sources including parents, school, and friends. However, they are particularly likely to remember the lessons that video games teach them. The active participation, repetition, and rewards that occur in video games make them a very effective teaching tool. In a 2009 statement the American Academy of Pediatrics (AAP) explains that children learn by observing a behavior and then trying it. The AAP maintains, "Video games provide an ideal environment in which to learn violence." It adds, "They place the player in the role of the aggressor and reward him or her for successful violent behavior."[24] And when youths play the games for long periods of time, the repetition increases the effect of the games. The AAP believes that video game violence is more harmful than that in other media, such as television, because players are actively participating in the violence.

> "Video games provide an ideal environment in which to learn violence."[24]
>
> —The American Academy of Pediatrics, an organization that works to improve children's health.

Desensitizing Youths

In addition to normalizing and reinforcing violent behavior, violent game play desensitizes youths to violence. The first time a young player shoots a person in a video game it may seem shocking and even upsetting. After playing the game for a while and shooting hundreds of people, the player becomes desensitized; the violence does not provoke much of a reaction.

A Majority Believes Violent Games Harm Youths

This chart shows the results of a poll conducted in 2013, concerning Americans' attitudes toward the effects of video game violence on youths. It shows that the majority of adults from all age groups, both male and female, believe violent video games lead to violent behavior by teen players.

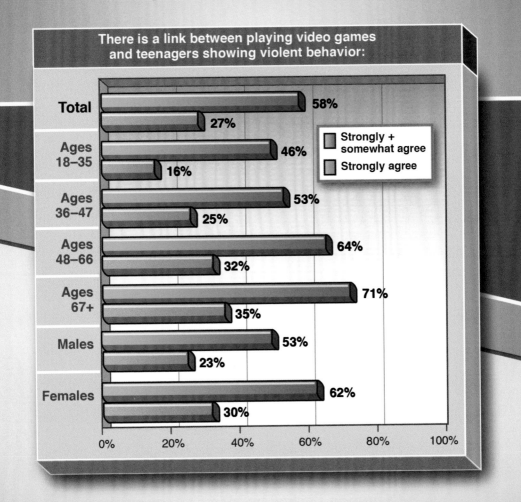

There is a link between playing video games and teenagers showing violent behavior:

- Total: 58% / 27%
- Ages 18–35: 46% / 16%
- Ages 36–47: 53% / 25%
- Ages 48–66: 64% / 32%
- Ages 67+: 71% / 35%
- Males: 53% / 23%
- Females: 62% / 30%

Legend:
- Strongly + somewhat agree
- Strongly agree

Source: Harris Interactive poll, "Majority of Americans See Connection Between Video Games and Violent Behavior in Teens," Harris Interactive, February 13, 2013. www.harrisinteractive.com.

It may even seem like normal behavior. Many players who become desensitized to violence in games may also become desensitized to violence in the real world. Brad J. Bushman observed this during his extensive laboratory research on the effects of violent video games. Bushman reports, "What we found is for people who were exposed to a lot of violent video games, their brains did not respond to the violent images. They were numb."[25]

Critics of game violence argue that when youths are desensitized to violence they are more likely to commit violent acts and also less likely to feel empathy for others. In 2013 fifteen-year-old Nehemiah Griego of Albuquerque, New Mexico, shot and killed his mother and father and his three younger siblings. Some media violence critics argue desensitization played a role. Investigators reported that he was unemotional when discussing the murders. Prior to his arrest, he even texted a picture of his mother's dead body to his girlfriend. Griego reportedly enjoyed playing violent video games, and while the reason for the shootings remains unclear, some critics believe this violent play may have helped desensitize him to the horrific act of shooting his five family members. Albuquerque psychologist Victor Strasburger argues, "I think parents are absolutely out of their minds if they let young children and teens play these games. They desensitize kids to the act of killing. They put you in the role of shooter, and they reward you for killing."[26]

> "I think parents are absolutely out of their minds if they let young children and teens play these [violent games] games. They desensitize kids to the act of killing. They put you in the role of shooter, and they reward you for killing."[26]
>
> —Victor Strasburger, a psychologist in Albuquerque, New Mexico.

An Opinion Backed by Major Organizations

A number of well-known organizations, whose goals include advocating for children's health, have made official statements cautioning that violent game play poses a risk for youths. The American Academy of Child & Adolescent Psychiatry (AACAP), the AAP, and APA have all cautioned that violent video games may be harmful to youths. These are all large and respected organizations with many experts among their membership. AACAP lists a large number of negative effects from video game violence. It says, "Studies of children exposed to violence have shown that they can become 'immune' or numb to the horror of violence, imitate the violence they see, and show more aggressive behavior with greater exposure to violence. Studies have also shown that the more realistic and repeated the exposure to violence, the greater the impact on children."[27]

Likewise, AAP says, "Exposure to violence in media, including television, movies, music, and video games, represents a significant risk to the health of children and adolescents."[28] Based on evidence that game violence may be harmful to youths, in 2005 the APA issued a resolution advocating for the reduction of violence in video games.

Video game violence is harmful to youths. It teaches them that violence is an acceptable way to behave, and it desensitizes them to violent behavior in the real world. Because of the proven potential for harm, a number of major scientific institutions advise caution for youths playing violent video games.

Video Game Violence Does Not Harm Youths

"A child playing a violent video game does not necessarily increase the likelihood that he or she will engage in real violence at that age or later in life."

—Bezio is an assistant professor at the University of Richmond's Jepson School of Leadership Studies.

Kristin M.S. Bezio, "Stop Blaming Video Games for America's Gun Violence," *Christian Science Monitor*, February 12, 2013. www.csmonitor.com.

Consider these questions as you read:

1. Do you agree with the argument that violent game play is an important part of social development for youths? Why or why not?
2. Do you think youths could engage in bonding and beneficial social interaction just as successfully with nonviolent video games as with violent ones? Explain your answer.
3. How persuasive is the argument that youths can easily distinguish between violent game play and acceptable behavior in the real world? Explain.

Editor's note: The discussion that follows presents common arguments made in support of this perspective, reinforced by facts, quotes, and examples taken from various sources.

Anytime teens or young adults commit violent acts—especially mass shootings—politicians, members of the media, and others immediately search for a link to video games. The topic of video games came up soon after twenty-year-old Adam Lanza shot and killed twenty-six people at Sandy Hook Elementary School in Newtown, Connecticut, in December 2012. The media reported that Lanza had played the game *Call of Duty*, which led to the assumption that game play must have been a factor in the shooting. For instance, New Jersey governor Chris Christie said, "You cannot tell me that a kid sitting in a basement for hours playing Call of Duty and killing people over and over and over again does not desensitize that child to the real life effects of violence."[29]

Despite comments like this, there is no evidence that Lanza's game play harmed him or influenced him to carry out the shooting. Christopher J. Ferguson argues that fears about violent video games having harmful effects on youths have persisted for years, but there is no evidence to support these fears. He says, "Ten years ago, scholars and politicians raised the possibility that such games might contribute to school shootings or other youth violence. What happened to these concerns? Quite simply, the research just hasn't panned out."[30]

Part of Healthy Development

Despite widespread concern about the effect of violent video games on youths, the fact is that violence has been a feature of children's entertainment for hundreds of years. Fairy tales, for example, are notoriously violent. *Hansel and Gretel* and *Little Red Riding Hood* are just two examples of stories that threaten children with being eaten.

Some experts argue that exposure to violence such as that in stories and video games is actually an important part of healthy development for youths and can have a number of positive effects. One benefit of exposure to pretend violence is that it helps youths learn to cope with anxiety and fear. Experts point out that violence is a normal and inescapable part of life. They contend that children will be better equipped to thrive if they learn how to deal with it. Experiencing violence in video games is a safe and controlled way of doing so. Cheryl K. Olson explains, "An attraction to violent and scary themes seems to be part of normal

> "Ten years ago, scholars and politicians raised the possibility that . . . [violent] games might contribute to school shootings or other youth violence. What happened to these concerns? Quite simply, the research just hasn't panned out."[30]
>
> —Christopher J. Ferguson, professor of psychology and criminal justice at Texas A&M International University.

33

development. Playing with those frightening images helps a child master the physical and emotional sensations that go with being afraid." She says, "Scary stories and games let children experience and deal with those feelings at a time and place where they know they are safe."[31]

Empowerment and Social Relationships

Playing violent video games can also be beneficial to youths because it can empower them. When children successfully face violence in a game, they feel powerful and in control. These feelings can carry over into the real world, bolstering self-esteem and helping them feel powerful and in control in real life too. For example, researcher Elena Bertozzi writes about how violent games can be used to empower girls. According to Bertozzi, predation games—in which the player is encouraged to hunt and kill in order to survive—have traditionally been played primarily by boys. However she believes that these types of games can empower girls by teaching them to face fear, accept challenges, and survive in stressful and aggressive environments. She argues that this empowerment can carry over into the real world and help women compete more successfully with men, for example in the job market. She says, "Encouraging females to play at the same kinds of digital games males do may finally affect female willingness to seek and achieve the same kinds of power and status of top males."[32]

Video games can also serve as an important way for youths to bond and to form social relationships. Some people see game play as a form of something called rough-and-tumble play, a kind of play-fighting where youths bond and establish relationships in social groups. Olson says, "Boys in particular often use rough-and-tumble play fighting to establish dominance and a social pecking order, with no intention to harm." According to Olson, "Video game play could serve as another arena for the developmentally appropriate battle for status among peers."[33] She believes that such play is a normal and necessary part of youths' social interaction.

Rough-and-tumble-play is only one of many types of beneficial social interactions that can occur in violent game playing. Matthew Chow is a psychiatrist and a gamer. He argues that video gaming encourages this beneficial social interaction because many games require players to interact

Video Games Have Many Positive Effects

Some people argue that rather than harming youth, video games—even violent ones—can actually have many positive effects. This chart shows data from a study of 1,254 seventh and eight grade students. While these youths reported playing numerous games, researchers found that the most popular game among the boys—and one of the most popular among the girls—was the violent *Grand Theft Auto* series. The chart reveals the percentage of youths who strongly agreed with various reasons for playing these games. It reveals that many of the reasons reported are positive, such as learning new things and interacting with friends.

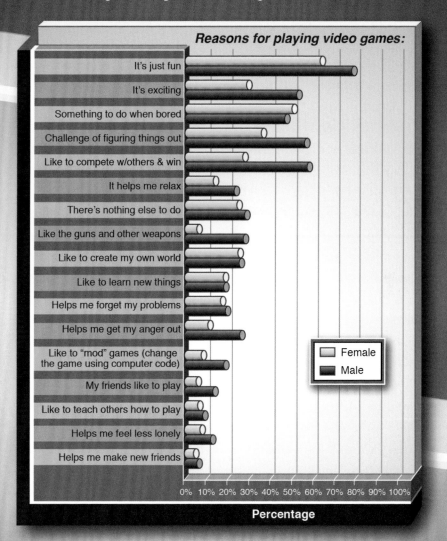

Reasons for playing video games:

It's just fun
It's exciting
Something to do when bored
Challenge of figuring things out
Like to compete w/others & win
It helps me relax
There's nothing else to do
Like the guns and other weapons
Like to create my own world
Like to learn new things
Helps me forget my problems
Helps me get my anger out
Like to "mod" games (change the game using computer code)
My friends like to play
Like to teach others how to play
Helps me feel less lonely
Helps me make new friends

Female
Male

0% 10% 20% 30% 40% 50% 60% 70% 80% 90% 100%

Percentage

Source: Cheryl K. Olsen, "Children's Motivations for Video Game Play in the Context of Normal Development," *Review of General Psychology*, vol. 14, no. 2, June 2010. www.apa.org.

with other people. Chow says that while in the past video games may have encouraged antisocial behavior because they were played alone, now the opposite is true. He says, "People join online communities populated by tens of thousands of individuals around the world. They participate in pro-social behaviors such as cooperative play, trading, negotiating, forming alliances, and creating rules of conduct. You need to be able to get along with a diverse community in order to succeed in online play."[34] Such play helps people to similarly conduct successful social interactions in the real world.

Releasing Aggression Safely

Yet another benefit of violent game play is that it lets youths release their aggression without actually harming anybody. Psychology professor and media expert Steven J. Kirsh points out that while aggression is a natural feeling that everybody experiences at some time, children are often taught that it is not appropriate to be aggressive. For example, he says, they may be told: "'People are for hugging, not hitting!' 'It's OK to be angry; it's not OK to hit!' 'I told you not to hit your sister! Time-out!'" According to Kirsh, "As each of the above quotes illustrates, children are socialized to inhibit acts of aggression. Moreover, failure to show appropriate restraint often results in punishment."[35] Video game violence can be a way for youths to release their aggression without actually harming anybody and without getting punished for being aggressive. Olson looks at the data obtained from focus groups with children and finds that this is what appears to happen in many cases. She reports that many youths say playing violent games helps them vent anger and relieve stress.

Concerns about game violence teaching real-world violence are also unfounded. Most young people can distinguish between the fantasy world of game play and the real world. Ferguson says, "Fairly early on, children learn to distinguish between fantasy and reality, and their brains don't treat these phenomena the same." He says, "Santa Claus is a prime example. Despite not only their parents but all of society conspiring to lie to children about the reality of this fellow (complete with old men in red capes at the mall as 'evidence'), children can reason out the improbability of his existence by the mid-elementary years." Ferguson says,

"With those kinds of reasoning powers, kids can handle a video game that doesn't even claim to be real."[36]

When gamers talk about their experiences, many of their comments lend support to this argument that violent game play is merely a form of entertainment for them and that they recognize that it does not resemble reality. Jared Gable, a young gamer, says, "When I'm playing online with my friends on games like Call of Duty 4, I don't think of myself as shooting and killing my friends, [we're] just having fun and scoring some points."[37] Another gamer, who calls herself "Kasumi," also insists that players recognize that game play is only pretend. She talks about *Grand Theft Auto* in which players engage in high levels of violence, and says, "This is very obviously a game. It's an act. It's entertaining because it's so ridiculously unrealistic; **sometimes it's just fun to be something you're not for a little while**. Whether you're a thug or a soldier or even a farmer, playing pretend is just *fun*."[38]

> "Scary stories and games let children experience and deal with those feelings at a time and place where they know they are safe."[31]
>
> —Cheryl K. Olson, expert on media effects.

There is no evidence that violent video games harm youths. In fact, these games actually have many beneficial effects, such as teaching youths to deal with anxiety and fear and allowing them to release aggression without actually harming anybody.

Chapter Three

Are Violent Video Games a Cause of Mass Shootings?

Violent Video Games Are a Cause of Mass Shootings

- Violent games inspire mass shooters by normalizing and glamorizing violence.
- Games lead players to falsely believe that they can commit violent acts without any consequences.
- Violent games are an effective training tool for potential shooters.
- In individuals already prone to violence, violent games can greatly increase the chances of a shooting.

The Debate at a Glance

Violent Games Are Not to Blame for Mass Shootings

- The vast majority of violent game players do not commit mass shootings.
- People who focus on video games as the cause of terrible events such as mass shootings are misguided.
- Shootings occur due to a complex mix of personal problems, not simply because someone plays video games.
- Someone who could commit a mass shooting already has a violent personality; games do not make them violent.

Violent Video Games Are a Cause of Mass Shootings

"Not all violent gamers become mass killers. But these days, almost all nonterrorist mass shooters are violent gamers. The link is undeniable."

—Sperry is an investigative journalist and Hoover Institution media fellow.

Paul Sperry, "Restrict 'Columbine Simulators' and Violent Video Games Before Guns," www.investors.com, December 19, 2012. http://news.investors.com.

Consider these questions as you read:

1. Do you agree with the argument that video games make shooting other people seem normal and even glamorous? Explain.
2. How persuasive is the argument that video games help shooters train? Explain your answer.
3. Taking into account the facts and arguments presented in this discussion, how persuasive is the argument that violent games cause mass shootings? Which arguments provide the strongest support for this perspective, and why?

Editor's note: The discussion that follows presents common arguments made in support of this perspective, reinforced by facts, quotes, and examples taken from various sources.

On the morning of April 20, 1999, Columbine High School students Dylan Klebold and Eric Harris walked into their school with guns, knives, and bombs and opened fire on those inside. Their goal was to kill as many people as possible. Twelve students and one teacher died, and twenty-one more were injured in the shooting. Afterward, investigators discovered that the two teens spent large amounts of time playing violent video games such as the first-person shooter game *Doom*. Many people believe that these games were a major cause of the shooting. The families of some of the victims even filed a lawsuit against a number of companies that create violent games, arguing that they were partly responsible for what happened. The lawsuit states, "Absent the combination of extremely violent video games and these boys' incredibly deep involvement, use of and addiction to these games and the boys' basic personalities, these murders and this massacre would not have occurred."[39] The Columbine shooting is just one example of mass shooters who have spent large amounts of time to playing violent games. There are, sadly, other examples and this strongly suggests a connection between violent video games and mass shootings.

Encouraging Violence

Many violent games make shooting other people seem normal and even glamorous. In these games, violence is encouraged as an effective way to play, and violent acts such as shooting or hitting a person are often rewarded with incentives such as points. Author and journalist Tom Bissell believes that some games go too far in their encouragement of violence. In June 2012 Bissell attended a demonstration of a game called *Splinter Cell: Blacklist*. In one part of the game, the hero tries to get information from a man by twisting a knife in his clavicle. Bissell says he left "sick and infuriated" at the way this horrific act was portrayed; it came across as a perfectly acceptable and effective strategy for winning the game. He says, "We've arrived in a strange emotional clime when our popular entertainment frequently depicts torture as briskly effective rather than literally the worst thing one human being can do to another."[40]

> "We've arrived in a strange emotional clime when our popular entertainment frequently depicts torture as briskly effective rather than literally the worst thing one human being can do to another."[40]
>
> —Tom Bissell, author and journalist.

And that behavior is spilling over into real life. The influence of such games can be found in mass shootings. Analysis of past shootings reveals that a number of shooters may have dressed or acted like characters in video games, suggesting that they were imitating the games when they carried out the shootings. In some cases, shooters have even admitted that they were inspired by a game. For example, stepbrothers William Buckner and Joshua Buckner killed one person and wounded another in 2003 when they fired shotguns at vehicles driving on Interstate 40 near their home in Tennessee. After their arrest, the Buckners told investigators that they got the idea of shooting at cars from the game *Grand Theft Auto 3*—where players also shoot at people and cars.

A False Portrayal of Reality

As this case reveals, in addition to inspiring players to imitate game violence in real life, video games allow players to believe that such acts have no harmful consequences. The Buckner brothers insisted they did not intend to hurt anyone. Clearly, no one in a game experiences the tragic consequences that befell the victims in the Buckner case.

Video game play differs from most other types of play in that it fails to teach players about real life consequences. Author and soldier David Grossman explains how other types of play include learning about the consequences of violence. He says, "We played caps when we were kids. You all remember playing caps? We had toy guns. And I said, Bang, bang, I got you, Billy.' And Billy said, 'No, you didn't.' So, I smacked him with my cap gun. And he cried, and he went to his mama, and I got in *big* trouble. And you know what I learned? I learned that Billy is real. And when I hurt Billy, bad things are going to happen to me."[41]

In contrast, says Grossman, "In the violent video games, I blow Billy's stinkin' head off in explosions of blood, countless thousands of times. And do I get trouble? No. I get points." In Grossman's opinion, video games are harmful because they do not teach youths the crucial lesson of interacting without hurting others. He insists, "The purpose of play, is to learn *not* to hurt members of your society, and members of your own species."[42]

Training to Shoot

The influence of violent games in mass shootings is wide-ranging; for some they have become a vehicle for training. Commenting on an online

Reducing Media Violence Would Help Prevent Mass Shootings

A significant percentage of Americans believes that mass shootings could be prevented by a larger police presence in schools, by devoting more money to mental health, and by decreasing violence in video games and other media. These are the findings of a Gallup poll conducted four days after the December 2012 mass shooting at Sandy Hook Elementary School in Newtown, Connecticut.

Do you think each of the following would be a very effective, somewhat effective, or not effective approach to preventing mass shootings at schools?

	Very effective	Somewhat effective	Not effective	No opinion
Increasing the police presence at schools	53%	34%	12%	1%
Increased government spending on mental health screening and treatment	50%	34%	14%	2%
Decreasing the depiction of gun violence on TV, in movies, and in video games	47%	31%	20%	2%
Banning the sale of assault and semi-automatic guns	42%	21%	36%	1%
Having at least one school official at every school carry a gun for the school's protection	34%	30%	34%	2%
News media refusing to print or read the names of the person responsible for the shooting	27%	30%	40%	3%

Source: Gallup poll, "To Stop Shootings, Americans Focus on Police, Mental Health," December 19, 2012. www.gallup.com.

article about game violence, one gamer maintains that playing shooting games has increased his real-life skill with guns. He says, "I'm now 24, and I've been playing all sorts of video games for years now. . . . To be honest, I can actually shoot more accurately than almost everyone I know, and I have better anticipation and a faster reaction time when we're out shooting a moving target."[43]

This is most worrisome when the gamer is someone like Anders Behring Breivik, who killed sixty-nine people and wounded hundreds of others in a 2011 shooting in Norway. In a rambling fifteen-hundred-page manifesto, Breivik says that he used violent games to train for the shooting: "I see MW2 [*Modern Warfare 2*] more as a part of my training-simulation than anything else. . . . You can more or less completely simulate actual operations."[44]

An Important Factor

Clearly, not every individual who plays violent video games will go on to commit a mass shooting. However, for certain types of individuals, such as those who are already prone to violence, violent games can be an important factor that spurs them to go on a shooting rampage. Paul Boxer, associate professor of psychology and faculty fellow in criminal justice at Rutgers–Newark University admits, "There is not a single scientist working on these issues in the mainstream who would ever claim that violent video games alone cause mass shootings." He explains, "Violent behavior is known to be the result of multiple and interacting risk factors—including mental illness, child maltreatment, substance use and other negative influences."[45]

> **"Playing violent video games increases the chances that someone will engage in aggressive or even violent behavior."[46]**
>
> —Paul Boxer, associate professor of psychology and faculty fellow in criminal justice at Rutgers–Newark University.

But Boxer argues that while they are not the only factor, violent games are an important one. Many people believe that without violent games, some shootings might not occur. Boxer adds, "Adam Lanza might have played a lot of violent games, but that could not have been enough to drive him to do what he did. However, you can bet it helped. Because playing violent video games increases the chances that someone will engage in aggressive or even violent behavior."[46]

Violent video games do not cause everyone who plays them to go out and shoot people; however, they do bear some responsibility for mass shootings. These games normalize and glamorize violence and misinform players about the consequences of that violence. It is violent games that have inspired many people to commit mass shootings.

Violent Games Are Not to Blame for Mass Shootings

"There is no evidence linking violent games to mass shootings."

—Ferguson is chair of the psychology and communication department at Texas A&M International University. He is the author of the novel *Suicide Kings*.

Christopher J. Ferguson, "Video Games Didn't Cause Newtown Rampage," CNN, February 20, 2013. www.cnn.com.

Consider these questions as you read:

1. Do you agree with the argument that there is no evidence that violent games cause mass shootings? Why or why not?
2. When Adam Lanza killed twenty-six people in a 2012 shooting, the media was quick to point out that he played violent video games. Why do you think the media is so quick to blame game violence for mass shootings?
3. How strong is the argument that violent people are drawn to violent game play, not made violent by it? Explain.

Editor's note: The discussion that follows presents common arguments made in support of this perspective, reinforced by facts, quotes, and examples taken from various sources.

Violent video games often get the blame for mass shootings and other violence, but an examination of the facts shows the fallacy of this position. There are millions of gamers around the world who spend millions of dollars on violent video games and countless hours playing them. Yet of all those millions, only a few individuals commit horrific crimes such as mass shootings. In the United States alone, as of July 2012, retail sales of *Call of Duty: Black Ops* had reached $16.4 million, and *Call of Duty: Modern Warfare 3* had reached $13.7 million, according to *Forbes*. However, according to the *Washington Post*, in 2012 there were a total of fourteen mass shootings in the United States. Of these, some of the shooters were found to have played violent games, while others had not. These figures show that only a small number of gamers have committed shootings and hundreds of thousands of others have not, disproving the theory that violent game play is to blame for mass shootings.

No Evidence of Causation

Even though critics continue to blame games, in reality there is only a small number of instances of a mass shooting having occurred following violent video game play, and even then there is no evidence that the shooting was caused by that play. In 2011 Anders Behring Breivik went on a shooting rampage in Norway, and at his trial he revealed that he played the violent game *Call of Duty* for hours a day. As a result, some people blamed that game for Breivik's actions. However journalist Paul Tassi says this conclusion makes no sense because millions of other people play that game without becoming killers. He writes, "To say that Call of Duty was a significant factor in these murders ignores the fact that there were probably 10 million COD players that did NOT go on a mass killing spree last year. In fact, only one did."[47]

Similar comments surfaced after the 2012 Newtown shooting committed by Adam Lanza. The media reported that Lanza had spent large amounts of time playing violent video games such as *Call of Duty*. While this might have been true, Cheryl K. Olson argues that thousands of other people play violent games and live normal lives without harming anybody. She points out that playing violent games is actually a common activity for a large percentage of teenagers and that most of these teenagers are not going on shooting sprees or committing any violent acts. She says, "It's true that the Newtown, Conn., shooter apparently played violent video games. But the local kids on your soccer team, your 13-year-old boys who live down the street from you, they're all playing these violent games, too, and they are probably OK."[48]

Journalist Max Fisher has investigated the link between video game play and gun-related murders in the world's ten largest game markets. His findings indicate that overall, there is no link between game playing and mass shootings. Fisher found that while the United States does have both a high level of gun-related murders and video game consumption, it is an exception to a larger trend. He says, "Other countries where video games are popular have much lower firearm-related murder rates. In fact, countries where video game consumption is highest tend to be some of the safest countries in the world."[49] These include Japan, the United Kingdom, Australia, France, and Germany—all of which are large consumers of video games but have relatively low rates of gun-related murders. Japan, for example, has almost no gun-related murders.

> "Countries where video game consumption is highest tend to be some of the safest countries in the world."[49]
>
> —Max Fisher, journalist.

Looking for an Answer

One reason video games are often blamed for mass shootings is that they provide an easy, if inaccurate, answer to why the shootings might have happened. When a mass shooting occurs, a natural reaction that people have is to look for a cause so that they can understand why it happened and try to prevent another in the future. Matt Peckham, who writes about video games for *Time* magazine, says, "When horrible things happen, we look for simple answers, for easy rationalizations—ways to essentially say, Oh, this is why so-and-so did such-and-such. We want the 'why' right now."[50] When it is discovered that a mass shooter also played a video game in which play included shooting people, the video game often becomes such an easy answer for society.

Researchers have noticed that society is often quick to blame violent games after mass shootings occur, even when there is no proof of their connection to the shooting. Tassi argues that people are far less likely to blame many other potential causes, such as the availability of guns. For example, Breivik's shooting quickly resulted in calls to ban violent video games. However, Tassi points out, "If he went to a gun range every single day for the past year . . . would we be talking about how shooting ranges are to blame? Would we want them all closed down for fear someone else might learn how to shoot a gun and kill someone?"[51]

No Link Between Video Games and Shootings

If video game violence were an influential factor in real-world violence, including mass shootings, one would expect to see a large number of gun-related killings in the world's top-ten video game markets. These graphs demonstrate that this is not the case. The first graph shows that most countries with high levels of spending on video games have low levels of gun-related murder. The second graph shows what the trend line should look like if a correlation actually existed between video games and shootings.

Gun-related murders and video game consumption

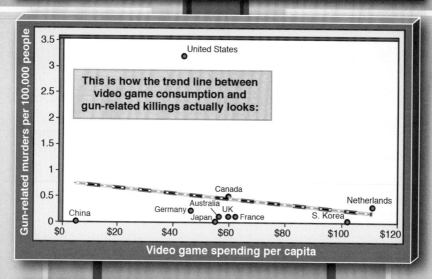

This is how the trend line between video game consumption and gun-related killings actually looks:

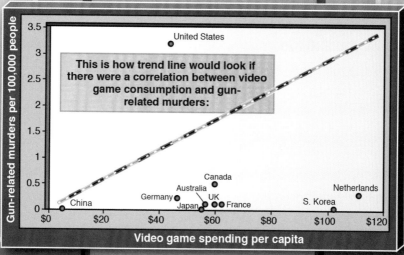

This is how trend line would look if there were a correlation between video game consumption and gun-related murders:

Source: Max Fisher, "Ten-Country Comparison Suggests There's Little or No Link Between Video Games and Gun Murders," *Washington Post*, December 17, 2012. www.washingtonpost.com.

In reality, there is no easy answer for why mass shootings occur. Addressing the desire to connect Breivik's shooting and his violent game play, Peckham cautions, "Reality . . . is far more complex."[52] The existing research has not proved a clear link between violent games and violent behavior. In fact, it shows that violent acts such as shooting are the result of a combination of many factors such as personality, mental problems, and family relationships. Tassi says, "Some individuals are simply mentally ill, sociopathic or both, and will find a way to kill people if they are determined enough."[53] In the case of such individuals, whether they play violent games is unlikely to determine whether they will commit a shooting. The ESA warns, "Having someone or something to blame is convenient, especially after an incident of terrible and unexplainable violence. However, to do so is simplistic, and more importantly, it is wrong."[54]

A Symptom of a Violent Personality

Some research shows that mass shooters are not made violent by their game play but instead are already violent individuals who are simply drawn to violent game play because of their personalities. James Alan Fox, Lipman Professor of Criminology, Law, and Public Policy at Northeastern University, argues that violent people are often drawn to violent entertainment, and thus it is not surprising to find that many mass shooters have also played violent video games. However, he says, "The ability to document a causal link—that consuming violent entertainment leads to violent behavior—has eluded social scientists for years." Instead, Fox argues, "Preoccupation with video games, although hardly healthy, is more a symptom of personal problems than a cause of them."[55]

> "The ability to document a causal link—that consuming violent entertainment leads to violent behavior—has eluded social scientists for years."[55]
>
> —James Alan Fox, Lipman Professor of Criminology, Law, and Public Policy at Northeastern University.

Fox discusses the example of Adam Lanza who shot and killed twenty-six people at Sandy Hook Elementary School in Connecticut in 2012.

Many people have argued that violent game play was to blame for Lanza's actions; however, Fox states that Lanza's attraction to violent games was a symptom of problems he was experiencing, not a cause of them. He says, "It was his social awkwardness and reclusiveness that impacted both his spending long hours playing games and his desire to strike back against a society that he perceived as unwelcoming."[56]

There is no evidence that violent video games are to blame for mass shootings. Most people who play violent games do not commit shootings, and researchers have found that those players who have carried out shootings were influenced by many other factors.

Chapter Four

How Should Video Game Violence Be Regulated?

Video Game Violence Should Be Strictly Regulated

- The video game industry does not sufficiently warn the public about the danger of violent games.
- Large numbers of children have easy access to violent games not intended for them.
- Parents need help monitoring their children's game play.
- Regulations to protect children would not violate the First Amendment.

The Debate at a Glance

Strict Regulation of Violence in Video Games Is Not Needed

- The video game industry already does an excellent job of regulating game violence.
- Research shows that the majority of retailers do not let minors rent or purchase violent games.
- Youths are exposed to violent game content because their parents choose to allow it, not through lack of regulation.
- Regulation of video games would violate the First Amendment.

Violent Video Games Should Be Strictly Regulated

"The government should have the right to ban violent video games just as they have the right to tell everyone to drive 20 miles per hour in a school zone. This is a good use of government intervention in this case."

—Waliszewski is director of the Plugged In department for Focus on the Family, an organization that is dedicated to helping families thrive.

Bob Waliszewski, quoted in Alex Murashko, Twitter post, "Survey: Violent Video Game Sales to Children Should Be Illegal," *Christian Post*, July 6, 2011. www.christianpost.com.

Consider these questions as you read:

1. Do you agree with the argument that government regulation is the best way to protect children from exposure to harmful game violence? Why or why not?

2. How strong is the argument that parents need help monitoring their children's game play? Explain.

3. Taking into account the facts and arguments presented in this discussion, how persuasive is the argument that the government should regulate video games? Which arguments provide the strongest support for this perspective, and why?

Editor's note: The discussion that follows presents common arguments made in support of this perspective, reinforced by facts, quotes, and examples taken from various sources.

In 2007 Colorado teenagers Lamar Roberts and Heather Trujillo were babysitting Trujillo's seven-year-old half-sister Zoe Garcia when they kicked her, hit her, and slammed her to the floor. Shortly afterward, Garcia stopped breathing and died. Doctors found that she had more than twenty bruises on her body, a broken wrist, bleeding and swelling in the brain, and other internal bleeding. Prosecutors say Roberts and Trujillo were acting out moves from the violent video game *Mortal Kombat*. This game has been widely critiqued for its violent content and was banned for several years in Australia, banned in South Korea, and restricted in Germany. In its review of the game, the Australian Government Classification Review Board describes some of the moves a player can perform in the game to kill an opponent. In one such move, a player "thrusts knife into chest, lifts body on knife, spins body, holds up second knife to cut off spinning legs, arms and head and throws down torso." In another deadly move a player "grabs leg, tears leg off, beats opponent with leg and crushes head."[57] By most any measure, this game is a gruesome example of entertainment gone awry—and it had tragic consequences for little Zoe Garcia. Games like this must be subject to greater regulation.

Informing the Public

At present, video games are subject to voluntary regulation by the game industry; however, this system is not sufficient. One problem is that video game companies fail to adequately inform consumers about the potential harm of playing these games. Numerous studies have shown that game violence is a serious risk. Brian Wilcox, director of the Center on Children, Families, and the Law at University of Nebraska–Lincoln, says, "As a whole, the body of work in this area suggests that there is a genuine need for concern about high levels of exposure to violent video games."[58] However, many

> "As a whole, the body of work in this area suggests that there is a genuine need for concern about high levels of exposure to violent video games."[58]
>
> —Brian Wilcox, director of the Center on Children, Families, and the Law at the University of Nebraska–Lincoln.

people do not understand that violent video games have the potential to cause real harm. The government needs to institute stricter regulations to ensure public safety.

Congressmen Joe Baca of California and Frank Wolf of Virginia have repeatedly tried to introduce legislation that would require violent games to carry a warning that video game violence has been linked to aggressive behavior. They believe the game industry has been irresponsible, and for this reason the government needs to step in. Baca says, "The video game industry has a responsibility to parents, families, and to consumers—to inform them of the potentially damaging content that is often found in their products." However, he says, "They have repeatedly failed to live up to this responsibility."[59] Wolf echoes Baca, arguing that the government has a responsibility to warn the public about certain things that pose a known risk and that this includes violent games. He says, "Just as we warn smokers of the health consequences of tobacco, we should warn parents—and children—about the growing scientific evidence demonstrating a relationship between violent video games and violent behavior."[60]

This risk increases every year as video game technology continues to improve. Improving technology means that video games have become more and more realistic, and video game violence today is extremely lifelike. Steven J. Kirsh explains, "Video game technology has dramatically improved over the past three decades. Far from the abstract and stick-like representations of the human form of yesteryear, modern graphics render bodies that are authentic looking when whole and just as lifelike when holes have been ripped into them by bullets, arrows, and machetes."[61] As game violence becomes more lifelike, it has an even greater impact on players.

> "We should warn parents—and children—about the growing scientific evidence demonstrating a relationship between violent video games and violent behavior."[60]
>
> —Frank Wolf, US congressman from Virginia.

Too Many Children Playing Violent Games

Research reveals that large numbers of children are playing violent video games that are not intended for them. Stricter regulation is needed to prevent this from happening. Iowa senator Charles Grassley insists, "There are too many video games that celebrate the mass killing of innocent people—games that despite attempts at industry self-regulation find their way into the hands of children."[62] Anecdotes reveal that access to violent games is easy and very common. Large numbers of people discuss their game play in online forums, and many reveal that they were able to purchase and play violent games at a young age. For example, one player says, "I was bought the first GTA [*Grand Theft Auto*] when I was, what, 11? 12? 13? Somewhere around there."[63] Another game player says,

> My mom tried her hardest to make sure Mortal Kombat or Ninja Turtles never made it into my hands. . . . But, sadly for her, it was all for not. All her hard work to keep violent content from me. Forcing my dad to tape over [violent movie] Conan The Destroyer, making sure my young mind was never tarnished by a splash of blood from an uppercut was all undone in one fowl swoop when my friend across the street got Mortal Kombat 2 from his brother.[64]

According to a 2010 analysis of media consumption habits of 1,254 students in grades seven and eight, the most popular game series among boys and one of the most popular among girls is *Grand Theft Auto*, which is rated M—for ages seventeen and up. This game contains killings, beatings, and other graphic violence.

Worries about restrictions on freedom by government regulation of the video game industry are misguided. The government has a responsibility to protect children from harm, and it has instituted other types of regulation that restrict freedom in order to accomplish that goal. Video game laws would be no different. For example, there are various laws designed to protect children from pornography since it is generally recognized that exposure to pornography can cause children serious harm. Like pornography, video game violence has the potential to inflict lasting harm on children and should be strictly regulated to protect them. US senator Jay Rockefeller of West Virginia argues that, at present, children are not sufficiently protected from the violent content of video games. He says, "Some people still do not get it. They believe that violent video games are no more dangerous to young minds than classic literature or Saturday morning cartoons. Parents, pediatricians, and psychologists know better." He insists, "We need to do more."[65] He argues that if video game makers are not the ones to do it, then the government needs to step in.

Too Few Parents Monitor Children's Game Play

According to a Kaiser Family Foundation survey, a significant percentage of parents do not set rules about which video games their children can play or how long they can play them. Overall, among eight- to-eighteen-year-olds, only 30 percent of those surveyed said their parents had such rules about their video game play. This lack of parental rules has led calls for more stringent regulation of video games.

Percent who say their parents have rules about:

Among all		Age 8–10	11–14	15–18
Which video games they can play	30%	54%	33%	12%
How much time they can spend playing video games	30%	45%	31%	18%

Source: Victoria J. Rideout, Ulla G. Foehr, and Donald F. Roberts, "Generation M^2: Media in the Lives of 8- to 18-Year-Olds," Kaiser Family Foundation, January 2010. www.kff.org.

Parents Need Help

While parents are ultimately responsible for monitoring their children's game playing, this does not mean that regulation is unnecessary. Regulation is an important tool that helps parents monitor their children's video game play and protect them from harm. In a 2011 case, Supreme Court justice Stephen Breyer argues that while it is the job of parents to monitor their children, sometimes they need help. He says, "Today, 5.3

million grade school-age children of working parents are routinely home alone." As a result, he says, "It has, if anything, become more important to supplement parents' authority to guide their children's development." Breyer argues that game regulation does not violate the First Amendment protection of free speech but rather serves as a tool to help society protect children from harm. He says, "In my view, the First Amendment does not disable government from helping parents make such a choice here—a choice not to have their children buy extremely violent, interactive video games, which they more than reasonably fear pose only the risk of harm to those children."[66]

The current system of video game regulation is not sufficient to protect society from the potential harms of game violence. Too many people play violent games without being fully aware of the risk. Greater regulation is needed for the protection of society, particularly youths.

Strict Regulation of Violence in Video Games Is Not Needed

"Attempts to ban violent video games or restrict their sale have already been overturned by the Supreme Court. Moreover, the video game industry has actually done a vastly improved job at self-regulating over the last decade."

—Kain is a journalist who frequently writes about video games.

Erik Kain, "Chris Christie Is Right About Parents and Violent Video Games—but His Policy Is Wrong," *Mother Jones*, April 25, 2013. www.motherjones.com.

Consider these questions as you read:

1. How strong is the argument that the video game industry is already doing a good job of regulating video games? Which arguments provide the strongest support for this perspective, and why?
2. Do you agree that additional regulation will not prevent children from playing violent games because it is parents who are allowing children to play these games? Why or why not?
3. Do you think all violent video games should be a protected form of free speech? Explain your answer.

Editor's note: The discussion that follows presents common arguments made in support of this perspective, reinforced by facts, quotes, and examples taken from various sources.

Video game violence is already regulated by the video game industry. Under the current system, the ESRB assigns games an age-based rating and also a ratings summary that gives more specific information about the content of the game. The rating summary for *Call of Duty: Black Ops* illustrates how this system provides prospective players with detailed information about the game's content. Most versions of this game are

M-rated. The summary states: "This is a first-person shooter in which players control a U.S. soldier who works for the C.I.A. and participates in both well-known and secret events during the Cold War (e.g., skirmishes, stealth espionage, assassinations, and interrogations involving torture). Players use a wide variety of weapons such as pistols, rifles, machine guns, and explosives to injure/kill enemies. Combat can generate pools of blood and dismembered limbs." Also, according to the summary, "Players can use enemy bodies as human shields and execute them at close range. In one sequence, broken glass is placed into the mouth of a man while he is repeatedly punched, causing blood to spill from his mouth. Language such as "f**k," "b*tch," and "sh*t" can be heard in the dialogue."[67]

Any reasonable person who reads this summary will know immediately what sort of game this is and how much graphic violence it contains. Anything more than this seems unnecessary. This conclusion is borne out by surveys of the people who buy and play games; these surveys show that this system is widely understood and works well.

Accomplishing the Goal of Informing Parents

As the ESRB's director of communications Eliot Mizrachi explains, one of the main purposes of regulation is to inform parents so they can make a decision about what their children play, and this is exactly what ESRB's ratings system accomplishes. He says, "The purpose of the ESRB ratings is to provide parents with information about video games they're buying for their children and families, and what is most important is that our ratings are meeting consumers' expectations with respect to content and age-appropriateness." According to Mizrachi, "The latest consumer research shows that parents are overwhelmingly satisfied with the guidance that ESRB ratings provide."[68]

In 2012 the Entertainment Software Association reported that 85 percent of parents are aware of the ESRB rating system, and 98 percent believe it is either somewhat or very helpful in choosing games. The video game industry is already very well regulated, and Michael D. Gallagher, president of the ESA, insists that any further regulation is, "a solution in search of a problem."[69]

Investigations by the Federal Trade Commission (FTC) also confirm that the current system of regulation works well. Starting in 2000 the FTC carried out a number of investigations on the marketing of violent entertainment to children in the United States. In 2009, its most recent report, the FTC stated that the ESRB is doing a good job of rating its products. The FTC also found that retailers do a good job of preventing children from purchasing M-rated games. Overall, says the FTC, "The video game industry continues to do an excellent job of clearly and prominently disclosing rating information in television, print, and Internet advertising and on product packaging." It found that improvements can be made, but that the video game industry is doing a better job than some other entertainment providers. It says, "The video game industry outpaces the movie and music industries in the three key areas that the Commission has been studying for the past decade: (1) restricting target-marketing of mature-rated products to children; (2) clearly and prominently disclosing rating information; and (3) restricting children's access to mature-rated products at retail."[70]

> "The latest consumer research shows that parents are overwhelmingly satisfied with the guidance that ESRB ratings provide."[68]
>
> —Eliot Mizrachi, director of communications for the ESRB.

Parental Choice

While research does show that many youths play violent games, this is primarily because their parents choose to allow it. Research shows that in the majority of cases, parents understand the ratings system and give their permission for children to rent or buy violent games. Thus, stricter regulation will do little to change the situation since parents have ultimate control over the games their children play. In an article for the *Boston College Law Review*, Christopher Clements investigates the role of parents. He says that according to research, 89 percent of parents are involved in purchasing video games for their children. In addition, most retailers do not sell M-rated games to children, with the FTC reporting

Video Game Industry Regulation Is Effective

Research shows that the current system of voluntary industry regulation of video games is effective in preventing underage gamers from buying graphic games. The Federal Trade Commission periodically deploys undercover investigators (called mystery shoppers) to check on retailers' willingness to sell various media to underage buyers. The results of these investigations show increasing success in stopping underage purchasers who attempt to obtain M-rated video games. The results also show that industry regulation of video games has been more successful than similar regulation of films, DVDs, and CDs.

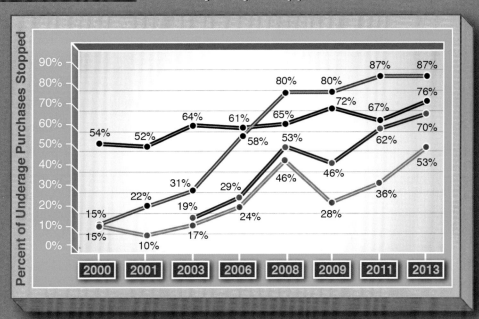

FTC Mystery Shopper Audits: 2000–2013

R-Rated Film   R-Rated DVD   PA-Labeled CD   M-Rated Video Game

Source: Entertainment Software Rating Board, "Consumer Research," 2013. www.esrb.org/about/awareness.jsp.

that 80 percent of underage children were refused. So, he concludes, "Taken together, these studies paint a curious picture of children playing games deemed inappropriate for their age purchased predominantly by their own parents." He says, "Because of this, there is little legislators can do, outside of completely banning the sale of violent video games, to keep them out of the hands of children."[71]

Chang Liu, a former game store employee, says that the store he worked in would not sell, rent, or trade M-rated games to anyone under age eighteen. However, in his experience this did not prevent these youths from eventually obtaining the game because most parents did not seem to mind their children having these games. He says, "Nearly half of all parents didn't care if what their kids were buying was mature or not. Most minors we turned away came back with a parent or relative over 18 who made never made a fuss about the purchase." Chang adds, "I've been yelled at on the phone by a mother for not selling her kids a mature game and how they were on spring break at home with nothing to do and she had to work during our business hours and we were horrible awful people for inconveniencing her."[72]

Protected by the Constitution

Critics of the video game industry have called on the government to ban certain violent game content or restrict access to that content by children. However, this would violate the First Amendment to the US Constitution, which guarantees the right to free speech for all Americans. Video games are a protected form of speech, and the government cannot make laws that restrict that speech just because someone believes it is harmful or offensive. Gallagher says, "As a medium, computer and video games are entitled to the same protections as the best of literature, music, movies, and art. In the end, Americans' rights to speech and expression are sacred and inviolate."[73]

The courts have repeatedly affirmed that video game content cannot be regulated by the government. According to the ESA, there are thirteen different court rulings stating that video games and computer games are protected speech and that legislative bodies cannot ban or limit access to them without violating the First Amendment to the Constitution. In 2011 the US Supreme Court struck down a California law that would have prohibited the sale of M-rated games to minors and fined retailers $1,000 for breaking the law. In its ruling the court maintains that there is no need for the government to regulate video game violence because there is no evidence that it actually causes harm to children. It points out that children are exposed to other types of violence without harm: for example they are given access to very violent books. Justice Antonin Scalia, writing for the majority, gives the example of books commonly read in high school: "Homer's Odysseus blinds Polyphemus the Cyclops by grinding out his eye with a heated stake. . . . In the Inferno, Dante and Virgil watch corrupt politicians struggle to stay submerged beneath a lake of boiling pitch, lest they be skewered by devils above the surface. . . . And Golding's Lord of the Flies recounts how a schoolboy called Piggy is savagely murdered by *other* children while marooned on an island."[74]

Not only would further regulation of video games be unconstitutional, but it is completely unnecessary. Research has repeatedly revealed that violent video games are already very well regulated by the game industry.

Source Notes

Overview: Video Games and Violence

1. Dan Nosowitz, "My Three Hours with the Most Violent Video-game," *Popular Science*, May 10, 2012. www.popsci.com.
2. Greg Casavin, "Manhunt Review," Gamespot, April 20, 2004. www.gamespot.com.
3. Shankar Vedantam, "It's a Duel: How Do Violent Video Games Affect Kids?," National Public Radio, July 7, 2011. www.npr.org.
4. Quoted in Beth Azar, "Virtual Violence," *Monitor on Psychology*, December 2010. www.apa.org.

Chapter One: Does Video Game Violence Cause Violent Behavior?

5. Brad J. Bushman, "Do Violent Video Games Increase Aggression?," *Psychology Today*, January 27, 2012. www.psychology today.com.
6. Craig A. Anderson et al., "Violent Video Game Effects on Aggression, Empathy, and Prosocial Behavior in Eastern and Western Countries: A Meta-Analytic Review," *Psychological Bulletin*, vol. 136, no. 2, 2010, p. 171.
7. Media Violence Commission of the International Society for Research on Aggression, "Aggressive Behavior," *Report of the Media Violence Commission*, vol. 38, 2012. www.wiley.com.
8. Jeanne Nagle, *Violence in Movies, Music, and the Media.* New York: Rosen, 2009, p. 37.
9. Nagle, *Violence in Movies, Music, and the Media*, p. 37.
10. Craig A. Anderson and Wayne A. Warburton, "The Impact of Violent Video Games: An Overview," in Wayne Warburton and Danya Braunstein, eds., *Growing Up Fast and Furious: Reviewing the Impacts of Violent and Sexualised Media on Children.* Annandale, NSW, Australia: Federation, 2012, p. 71.
11. Quoted in Joshua Gardner, "Do Video Games Make Kids Violent?," *ABC News*, December 17, 2012. http://abcnews.go.com.

12. Quoted in Azar, "Virtual Violence."

13. Simon Egenfeldt-Nielsen, Jonas Heide Smith, and Susana Pajares Tosca, *Understanding Video Games: The Essential Introduction*. New York: Routledge, 2013, p. 266.

14. Egenfeldt-Nielsen, Smith, and Tosca, *Understanding Video Games*, p. 270.

15. Christopher J. Ferguson, "The Wild West of Assessment: Measuring Aggression and Violence in Video Games," in Leonard Annetta and Stephen Bronack, eds., *Serious Educational Game Assessment: Practical Methods and Models for Educational Games, Simulations and Virtual Worlds*. Netherlands: Sense, 2010, p. 31.

16. Michael D. Gallagher, "Video Games Don't Cause Children to Be Violent," *U.S. News & World Report*, May 10, 2010. www.usnews.com.

17. Erik Kain, "As Video Games Sales Climb Year Over Year, Violent Crime Continues to Fall," *Forbes*, April 19, 2012. www.forbes.com.

18. A. Scott Cunningham, Benjamin Engelstätter, and Michael R. Ward, "Understanding the Effects of Violent Video Games on Violent Crime," Social Science Research Network, April 7, 2011. http://ssrn .com.

19. Cheryl K. Olson, "Children's Motivations for Video Game Play in the Context of Normal Development," *Review of General Psychology*, vol. 14, no. 2, p. 182.

Chapter Two: How Does Video Game Violence Affect Youths?

20. Brandon Keim, "What Science Knows About Video Games and Violence," PBS, February 28, 2013. www.pbs.org.

21. Media Violence Commission, "Aggressive Behavior."

22. Media Violence Commission, "Aggressive Behavior."

23. David Ropeik, "The Aurora Shootings and the Mean World Syndrome," *Huffington Post*, July 25, 2012. www.huffingtonpost.com.

24. American Academy of Pediatrics, "Policy Statement—Media Violence," 2009. www.psychology.iastate.edu.

25. Quoted in Shankar Vedantam, *Morning Edition*, National Public Radio, July 7, 2011. www.npr.org.

26. Victor Strasburger, "Parents 'Out of their Minds' to Allow Violent Games, Psychologist Says," KOAT, Albuquerque, January 24, 2013. www.koat.com.

27. American Academy of Child & Adolescent Psychiatry, "Children and Video Games: Playing with Violence," *Facts for Families*. March 2011. www.aacap.org.

28. American Academy of Pediatrics, "Policy Statement—Media Violence."

29. Quoted in Charlie Spiering, "Chris Christie Goes After 'Call of Duty' Video Games," *Washington Examiner*, January 9, 2013, http://washingtonexaminer.com.

30. Christopher J. Ferguson, "Video Games Don't Make Kids Violent," *Time*, December 7, 2011. www.time.com.

31. Cheryl K. Olson, "Children's Motivations for Video Game Play in the Context of Normal Development," *Review of General Psychology,* vol. 14, no, 2, p. 185. www.apa.org.

32. Quoted in Kyle Prahi, "University Author Argues That Games 'Where You Must Kill to Survive' Are Good for Female Children," Playstation Universe, February 14, 2013. www.psu.com.

33. Olson, "Children's Motivations for Video Game Play," p. 185.

34. Quoted in Winda Benedetti, "Worried About Your Child's Gaming: Psychiatrists Say 'Play with Them,'" *NBC News*, December 20, 2012, www.nbcnews.com.

35. Steven J. Kirsh, *Children, Adolescents, and Media Violence: A Critical Look at the Research.* Los Angeles: Sage, 2012, p. 83.

36. Ferguson, "Video Games Don't Make Kids Violent."

37. Quoted in Debatewise, "Violent Video Games, Music and Films Are Resulting in an Increase of Violent Behavior and Crimes in the Real World." http://debatewise.org.

38. Kasumi, "Why Do We Like Violence, Anyway?," IGN, January 21, 2013. www.ign.com.

Chapter Three: Are Violent Video Games a Cause of Mass Shootings?

39. Quoted in *USA Today*, "Columbine Lawsuit Targets Video Game-makers," February 6, 2002. http://usatoday30.usatoday.com.

40. Tom Bissell, "Thirteen Ways of Looking at a Shooter," *Grantland*, July 12, 2012. www.grantland.com.

41. David Grossman, "Violent Video Games Are Mass-Murder Simulators," *Executive Intelligence Review*, April 27, 2007. www.larouchepub.com.

42. Grossman, "Violent Video Games Are Mass-Murder Simulators."

43. PenguinBurrito, comment on "How Do We Stop the Next Sandy Hook? Glenn Talks with Dave Grossman About Gun Violence in Schools," Glenn Beck, January 3, 2013. www.glennbeck.com.

44. Quoted in John Gaudiosi, "Norway Suspect Used *Call of Duty* to Train for Massacre," *Forbes*, July 24, 2011. www.forbes.com.

45. Paul Boxer, "Do Violent Video Games Breed Violent Behavior? Yes." *NJ.com* (blog), April 30, 2013. http://blog.nj.com.

46. Paul Boxer, "Do Violent Video Games Breed Violent Behavior? Yes."

47. Paul Tassi, "The Idiocy of Blaming Video Games for the Norway Massacre," *Forbes*, April 19, 2012. www.forbes.com.

48. Quoted in Jeffrey Brown, "Can Violent Video Games Play a Role in Violent Behavior?," PBS, February 19, 2013. www.pbs.org.

49. Max Fisher, "Ten-Country Comparison Suggests There's Little or No Link Between Video Games and Gun Murders," *Washington Post*, December 17, 2012. www.washingtonpost.com.

50. Matt Peckham, "Norway Killer Played *World of Warcraft*, Which Probably Means Nothing at All," *Time*, April 17, 2012. www.time.com.

51. Tassi, "The Idiocy of Blaming Video Games."

52. Matt Peckham, "Norway Killer Played *World of Warcraft*."

53. Tassi, "The Idiocy of Blaming Video Games."

54. Entertainment Software Association, "Essential Facts About Games and Violence," 2011. www.theesa.com.

55. James Alan Fox, "Expert: Banning Violent Video Games Would Do Little to Avert the Next Mass Murder," *New York Daily News*, March 24, 2013. www.nydailynews.com.

56. Fox, "Expert: Banning Violent Video Games Would Do Little."

Chapter Four: How Should Video Game Violence Be Regulated?

57. Australian Government Classification Review Board, "Review of the Board's Decision to Classify the Computer Game *Mortal Kombat* RC, 11 March, 2011." www.classification.gov.au.

58. Quoted in Azar, "Virtual Violence."

59. Joe Baca, "Baca Sponsors Bill Mandating Video Games Be Sold with Warning Labels," press release, Congressman Joe Baca, March 19, 2012. http://baca.house.gov.

60. Frank Wolf, "Baca Sponsors Bill Mandating Video Games Be Sold with Warning Labels."

61. Kirsh, *Children, Adolescents, and Media Violence*, p. 229.

62. Quoted in Brenden Sasso, "Grassley: Voluntary Ratings for Violent Video Games Not Enough," *The Hill*, January 13, 2013. http://the hill.com.

63. "Marter," comment on "ESRB Ratings When You Were a Kid," *Escapist*, September 24, 2012. www.escapistmagazine.com.

64. "Chester Rabbit," comment on "ESRB Ratings When You Were a Kid," *Escapist*, September 24, 2012. www.escapistmagazine.com.

65. Jay Rockefeller, "Rockefeller Introduces Bill to Study Violent Video Games Impact on Children," press release, Jay Rockefeller for West Virginia, December 19, 2012. www.rockefeller.senate.gov.

66. Stephen Breyer, dissenting opinion, *Brown, Governor of California, et al. v. Entertainment Merchants Association et al.* US Supreme Court, June 27, 2011.

67. Entertainment Software Rating Board, "Call of Duty: Black Ops," Rating Summary. www.esrb.org.

68. Eliot Mizrachi, interview by Ryan Rigney, "Opinion: On *Halo: Reach*'s M Rating and the ESRB," Gamasutra, March 9, 2011. www.gama sutra.com.

69. Gallagher, "Video Games Don't Cause Children to Be Violent."

70. Federal Trade Commission, "Marketing Violent Entertainment to Children: A Sixth Follow-Up Review of Industry Practices in the Motion Picture, Music Recording & Electronic Game Industries," December 2009. www.ftc.gov.

71. Christopher Clements, "Protecting Protected Speech: Violent Video Game Legislation Post–*Brown v. Entertainment Merchants Ass'n.*," *Boston College Law Review*, vol. 53, no. 2. http://lawdigitalcommons .bc.edu.

72. Quoted in Nadia Oxford, "ESRB Ratings: Do They Work?" *Game Theory*, September 21, 2010. http://gametheoryonline.com.

73. Gallagher, "Video Games Don't Cause Children to Be Violent."

74. Antonin Scalia, majority opinion, *Brown, Governor of California, et al. v. Entertainment Merchants Association et al.* US Supreme Court, June 27, 2011.

Video Games and Violence Facts

Players

- According to the ESA, in 2012 the average game player was thirty years old. Only 32 percent of players were under eighteen.
- In a 2010 report the Kaiser Family Foundation reports that eight- to eighteen-year-olds spent an average of 1:13 hours playing video games every day.
- In a 2011 survey of 4,136 children, the research firm NPD Group found that 91 percent of children between ages two and seventeen played video games.
- The Entertainment Merchant's Association reports that in 2010 consumers spent $25.1 billion on video games, hardware, and accessories.
- According to a 2011 report by the *Huffington Post*, more than 46 million households in the United States have at least one video-gaming system.

Violent Games

- According to the Entertainment Merchant's Association, 76 percent of all games sold in 2010 were rated "E" for Everyone, "T" for Teen or "E10+" for Everyone 10+.
- According to a 2011 report by *USA Today*, approximately 5 percent of video games are in the M category, but they account for a quarter of all video game sales.
- The Entertainment Software Association reports that in 2011, 18.4 percent of games sold were shooter games.
- According to a 2010 report by the Kaiser Family Foundation, more than half of eight- to eighteen-year-olds said they had played the violent game *Grand Theft Auto*.

- In a study published in the *Journal of Experimental Social Psychology* in 2011, researchers from the University of Missouri report that in a study of seventy young adults, violent game play desensitized people to violence: those who played violent games for twenty-five minutes had a smaller brain response when exposed to violent images than those who played nonviolent games.

Positive Effects

- According to a 2012 report by the Entertainment Software Association, 52 percent of parents believe video games are a positive part of their child's life.
- In 2010 Christopher J. Ferguson and Stephanie M. Rueda published the results of a study of 103 young adults: the researchers found that violent video game play not only had no impact on aggressive behavior, but it also reduced depression and hostile feelings in players.
- In a 2013 poll of 2,278 US adults, research firm Harris Interactive found that 69 percent believed that playing video games is a good thing for children because it can help with hand/eye coordination and provide other skills.
- In a 2010 article in the *Review of General Psychology*, Cheryl K. Olson reports that in her research of 1,254 students in grades seven and eight, 45 percent of boys and 20 percent of girls reported that they used video games to help them cope with anger.

Regulation

- According to a 2011 poll of one thousand American adults by Rasmussen Reports, two out of three people believed that state governments should be allowed to prohibit the sale or rental of violent video games to minors.
- Based on research done in 2012, the ESA reports that 88 percent of parents believe that their rating system is "very helpful" or "somewhat helpful."
- In a 2013 undercover investigation, the Federal Trade Commission found that only 13 percent of underage shoppers were able to purchase M-rated video games from retailers.

- According to a 2013 poll by research firm Harris Interactive, which interviewed 2,278 US adults, 38 percent said they knew nothing about the video game ratings system.
- In a 2012 Gallup poll of 1,009 adults, 47 percent of people said that reducing the depiction of gun violence in television, movies, and video games would be a very effective way to prevent another mass shooting at a school.
- According to a 2011 CNN report, at least nine US states have had their attempts to restrict video game content struck down by the courts.

Related Organizations and Websites

Center for Successful Parenting
PO Box 3794
Carmel, IN 46082
phone: (317) 581-5355
e-mail: csp@onrampamerica.net
website: www.sosparents.org

The Center for Successful Parenting believes that violence in the media, including video games, is harmful to the development of children. Its website contains news and research about the effects of media violence.

Common Sense Media
650 Townsend, Suite 435
San Francisco, CA 94103
phone: (415) 863-0600 • fax: (415) 863-0601
website: www.commonsensemedia.org

Common Sense media is a nonprofit organization that works to provide trustworthy information about media to kids and families. It believes families should have an informed choice about the media they consume. Its website has video game reviews and research.

Entertainment Consumers Association (ECA)
64 Danbury Rd., Suite 700
Wilton, CT 06897
phone: (203) 761-6180 • fax: (203) 761-6184
e-mail: feedback@theeca.com
website: www.theeca.com

The ECA is a nonprofit organization that represents video game players. It is opposed to the regulation of video games based on content and supports the current system of self-regulation by the game industry. Its website contains facts and position papers about video games.

Entertainment Software Association (ESA)

575 7th St. NW, Suite 300
Washington, DC 20004
website: www.theesa.com

The ESA is the trade association for the US computer and video game industry. Its website contains numerous research reports and facts and articles about video games.

Entertainment Software Rating Board (ESRB)

317 Madison Ave., 22nd Floor
New York, NY 10017
phone: (212) 759-0700
website: www.esrb.org

The ESRB is the nonprofit, self-regulatory body that assigns ratings for video games and apps so parents can make informed choices. Its website has information about the video game rating system and its enforcement.

International Game Developers Association (IGDA)

19 Mantua Rd.
Mount Royal, NJ 08061
phone: (856) 423-2990 • fax: (856) 423-3420
e-mail: contact@igda.org
website: www.igda.org

The IGDA is an industry association that promotes the interests of the people who create video games. It is opposed to censorship of games. Its website contains articles and reports about video games.

Media Smarts

950 Gladstone Ave., Suite 120
Ottawa, ON
Canada, K1Y 3E6
phone: (613) 224-7721 • fax: (613) 761-9024
e-mail: info@mediasmarts.ca
website: http://mediasmarts.ca

Media Smarts is a Canadian organization that works to educate young people so that they can develop critical thinking skills and be informed media users. Its website contains news, research, and articles about video games.

Parent Further
615 First Ave. NE, Suite 125
Minneapolis, MN 55413
phone: (800) 888-7828
e-mail: info@parentfurther.com
website: www.parentfurther.com

Parent Further provides research and education about the impact of media on children and families. Its website provides reviews of video games in addition to fact sheets and articles about their effects.

For Further Research

Books

Simon Egenfeldt-Nielsen, Jonas Heide Smith, and Susana Pajares Tosca, *Understanding Video Games: The Essential Introduction.* New York: Routledge, 2013.

Steven J. Kirsh, *Children, Adolescents, and Media Violence: A Critical Look at the Research.* Los Angeles: Sage, 2012.

Jeffrey Kottler, *The Lust for Blood: Why We Are Fascinated by Death, Murder, Horror, and Violence.* Amherst, NY: Prometheus, 2011.

Dorothy G. Singer and Jerome L. Singer, *Handbook of Children and the Media, 2nd ed.* Thousand Oaks, CA: Sage, 2011.

Periodicals

Craig A. Anderson et al. "Violent Video Game Effects on Aggression, Empathy, and Prosocial Behavior in Eastern and Western Countries: A Meta-Analytic Review," *Psychological Bulletin*, vol. 136, no. 2, 2010.

Brad J. Bushman, "Do Violent Video Games Increase Agression?," *Psychology Today*, January 27, 2012. www.psychology today.com.

Economist, "No Killer App; the Moral Panic About Video Games Is Subsiding," December 10, 2011.

Christopher J. Ferguson, "Blazing Angels or Resident Evil? Can Violent Video Games Be a Force for Good?," *Review of General Psychology*, vol. 14, no. 2, 2010.

Erik Kain, "Warning: These Congressmen Want to Legislate Away Your Free Speech with 'The Violence in Video Games Labeling Act,'" *Forbes*, March 30, 2012.

Internet Sources

Entertainment Software Association, "Essential Facts about Games and Violence," 2011. www.theesa.com/facts/pdfs/ESA_EF_About_Games_and_Violence.pdf.

Harvard Medical School, "Violent Video Games and Young People," *Harvard Mental Health Letter*, October 2010. www.health.harvard.edu/newsletters/Harvard_Mental_Health_Letter/2010/October/violent-video-games-and-young-people.

Shankar Vedantam, "It's a Duel: How Do Violent Video Games Affect Kids?," National Public Radio, July 7, 2011. www.npr.org/2011/07/07/137660609/its-a-duel-how-do-violent-video-games-affect-kids.

Index

Note: Boldface page numbers indicate illustrations.

Perkins County Schools
PO Box 829
Grant NE 69140-0829